STRIPED SCARVES
AND
COAL DUST

STRIPED SCARVES AND COAL DUST

BY

JENNI WYN HYATT

ILLUSTRATIONS BY CATHY KNIGHT

First published in 2019
by R. Haigh & Sons Publications

The right of Jenni Wyn Hyatt to be identified as author of
this work has been asserted in accordance with Section 77
of the Copyright, Designs and Patents Acts 1988

A CIP record for this book is available at the British Library

ISBN: 9 780 244 477 967

Jenni Wyn Hyatt, née Williams, was born in Maesteg in 1942. Her poetry has appeared in magazines such as *The Lyric, The Dawntreader, Aberystwyth EGO, Llais y Derwent, the Journal of the Society of Classical Poets,* the webzine *The Road Not Taken: A Journal of Formal Verse, Poetry24* online and elsewhere.

Her subjects include Wales, nature, the tragedy of war, childhood memories and the human condition, with a smattering of humorous verse. She writes usually, but not exclusively, using rhyme and metre and exploring a multiplicity of poetic forms. Her work is accessible to poets and non-poets alike.

Jenni's first collection, *Perhaps One Day,* was published by Rowanvale Books in 2017. Priced at £5.99, it is available directly from the publisher or from Amazon.

Contents

The title of this collection is taken from two of its poems, 'Maesteg Childhood' and the Welsh version of 'Old College, Aberystwyth', where the Welsh for 'striped scarves' is used in place of the English 'scarves of red and green'. It reflects my upbringing in Maesteg, which was then the centre of a coal-mining valley, and my time as a student in Aberystwyth, 1959 - 1963.

Heavily influenced by the 'Land of Song', may some of my poetry sing in your heart and speak to your soul.

In memory of my dear friend,

Reginald John Saville (Reg),

of Langton Matravers, Dorset,

choir master, organist,

illustrator, local historian,

June 30th 1922 to January 20th 2019

'Love always, Jen xxxx'

Seasons

Summer Borders

Rambling roses clothe the fences,
scrambling sedums thrive below,
honeysuckle stirs the senses,
sunny-centred daisies glow.

Beds are multi-coloured palettes,
reds and yellows, purples, blues,
spilling over onto pathways,
thrilling with their vibrant hues.

Old-world pinks with clove-like fragrance,
bold nasturtiums, hollyhocks,
white gardenias' evening radiance,
bright pink panicles of phlox.

Calmness with your garden grows,
balm for turmoil, ease for woes.

First published in 'the Lyric', Summer 2018, 'Summer Borders' was subsequently chosen as the best poem in that issue because of the rhymes which occur at the beginnings and ends of the lines.

In Early October

Pale yellow ash keys dangle from green fingers
where withered husks of blackberries still linger.
Dark elderberries; spheres of guelder rose
mingle with jewelled reds of hips and haws -
deep leaves their firmament, their beauty vies
with stars that dazzle in cold midnight skies.
Hydrangea's leaves are richly tinged with rust,
her vibrant flowers crumbling, now, to dust.
Golden rudbeckias, blooming since July,
survey the changing scene with undimmed eye.

*This poem was written for Wendy Pratt's online
poetry course 'Season of Mists' in October 2018.*

October Sounds

As breezes strip the silver branches bare,
the crow grows more insistent from the birch,
redoubling his primeval raucousness.
The robin's song, September's shrill surprise,
wanes with the year, but softer, sweeter still,
his lonely voice will cheer winter's chill.

Where are the sounds of summer? Long departed.
Barbecue chatter, small children's laughter
will not be heard again until next May.
Mowers, blades oiled, are stashed away unseen,
redundant and recumbent they will lie
until the spring awakens blades of green.

*This poem was written for Wendy Pratt's online
poetry course 'Season of Mists' in October 2018.*

Autumn Shadows

Leaves shroud the path.
At dusk, lurking shadows
fox me like ghosts,

shadows of the past
foxing my memories,
fragile as leaves.

Fox crosses my path,
A living shadow,
leaf-russet.

*This poem was written for Wendy Pratt's online
poetry course 'Season of Mists' in October 2018.*

November Oak

At woodland's edge, a sorry sight;
in listless bunches sombre, brown,
lacklustre leaves hang limply down -
November oak, robbed of its might,

its Autumn foliage far eclipsed
by birch trees dancing yellow-gold,
the cherry tree in crimson clothed,
the scarlet hues of haws and hips,

but haloed by November's sun,
low in the sky, it's all aflame,
like Aslan with his fiery mane -
King of the Forest once again!

Snapshots on a Winter Walk

Snow-caped landscape.
Reflected sunlight
shimmers all around.

Silver-spangled stalks
and crystals crunch
on virgin ground.

Cerulean sky
and sapphire sea's
colours astound.

Forgotten leaves
float softly down
without a sound.

Visitor

Late January day of sky and sun,
The dogwood dressed to thrill in dragon red;
like swords from scabbards, crocuses emerge;
and, virginal, the snowdrops bow their heads.
I hear your 'Ribbit, ribbit' from afar
but it's a long time since you graced the bed
where roses grow – and where I place the oats
and raisins for the birds who come to feed.

The Alpha blackbird's here, fanned tail aloft;
with other males he squabbles over mates.
And then, to my delight, I see you land.
Your movements are so gentle, so sedate
amongst your chasing cousins' noisy band.
With soft brown back and arrow-speckled breast,
bright-eyed, you hop around and eat your fill,
my lucky song thrush, ever welcome guest.

The dogwood (cornus) is a shrub which has red stems in winter. The particular variety which we have in our garden is called 'Red Dragon'.

The song thrush is seen as a symbol of good luck in some European cultures.

People

and

Places

Borderland

Here in this borderland with savage past,
now mighty Offa's Dyke's a muddy ditch,
the Marcher Lords are silent effigies,
and Glyndwr's Way is but a walking path;

the ruined castles pose for scenic shots
and rape's a shriek of yellow in the fields,
the only turbulence the summer clouds,
which threaten rain.

                In every narrow lane,
the tumbling hedgerows brim with buttercups;
high hedges block the view as in a maze
and blur both time and place. Each byway leads

to quiet villages with cryptic names,
part English and part Welsh. The churches stand
wide open - and their Jacobean pews
still bear the faded names of local farms,

while, in the graveyards, lichen-covered stones
guard well their secrets. No-one now can tell
if saint or scoundrel, rich or poor man's bones
lie peacefully beneath this well-kept sod.

*First published in the anthology 'Best of British',
Paper Swans Press 2017.*

Dad's Box

I take it out from where I keep it safe
and open up my father's treasure chest,
a metal box with decorated lid,
in which he kept important documents
and souvenirs – his air raid warden's badge,
a photo of my Mum in pretty dress,
another of his friend, who died too young,
a lighter, a tie-pin, his father's pocket watch,
a battered groat (a coin worth four old pence),
a gold half sovereign, and he would impress,
"Sell this if you should be in dire straits" –
I often have been but I never would;
some names and numbers in his square strong hand
on scraps of paper; a bunch of tiny keys -
that open nothing now except my memories.

*This poem was written for Wendy Pratt's online
poetry course 'Season of Mists' in October 2018.*

*The small box in the poem belonged to my father,
Edgar Williams, 1905 to 1965.*

Dizain: The Isle of Man

Here Celtic crosses, chambered tombs,
and standing stones can open doors
connecting us with ancient times.
Here cobalt sea with greedy jaws
and foaming tongue assails your shores.
Here, round Snaefell the ravens ply
their twisting antics in the sky.
Here literature is vibrant still;
your bardic past will never die
while poets meet to share their skill.

*This poem was chosen to be part of the 'Poetry Puzzle'
on the Isle of Man, August 2017.*

Copper Lustre Jug

I've always known the jug of copper lustre,
a pretty thing that was my mother's pride;
now scarlet roses nestle there in clusters
their blooms reflected in its burnished sides.

Into the past reflection swiftly reaches -
the jug's filled with evaporated milk;
I see a cut glass bowl of crescent peaches,
a tablecloth that's worked in coloured silks.

Four people sitting round at tea on Sundays,
with bread and butter too and sometimes cake;
I'm grateful for a childhood full of fun days,
security that tough times could not shake.

Small things bring back my childhood every day.
Tomorrow … will my children feel this way?

Everlasting Rain

How I remember Queensland that October,
the Sunshine Coast obscured by a veil
which swept and swirled around us, and moreover,
disgorged on us its everlasting rain.

The hired campervan all new and gleaming
without a single hook or towel rail,
the puddles that we splashed through on the campsites,
the pounding, on the roof, of endless rain.

The butcherbird that woke us every morning,
the noisy miner birds – how close they came,
the charming pair of ducks that quacked and waddled
and wallowed in the unremitting rain.

The floods that closed the road and blocked our passage
to somewhere we will never go again,
the walks and trips of long anticipation,
all kyboshed by the driving, drenching rain.

The records that we found in Maryborough,
the slithering, on our ancestral trail,
in jacaranda petals on the pavement,
the Sunshine Coast – and amaranthine rain!

October 2017. See also the poem 'Prospecting'.

Maesteg Childhood 1948 – 1958

When I was six, I got a three-wheeled bike,
a sturdy one. I never called it 'trike' –
trikes were far smaller things, for little kids.
How we careered down Cemetery Road,
one steering, the other on the handlebars,
taking the bend into Turberville Street
at breakneck speed, or so it always seemed.
One time my cousin came to play; we struck
a bump and came to grief. I still have marks
of Maesteg's coal dust lurking in my knees.

Talking of battle scars, we were forbidden
to cross the railway line – "too dangerous,"
the adults said – and so we rushed across.
Twice in my guilty haste I tripped and fell,
the indentations showing faintly still.

One winter day, after a fall of snow,
the two of us of tricycle adventures
climbed Garth Mountain straight after junior school,
pretending to be grown-up mountaineers.
Apparently, although we didn't know,
all kinds of dangers lurked beneath the drifts –
we could have fallen into old mine shafts.
I faced my parents' wrath when I got home.

Then, at thirteen, I got a bicycle,
a proper bike, though very second-hand.

How good it felt, when summer breezes streamed
through hair. Sometimes we rode down to Cefn Ydfa Farm,
ruined home of Ann, poor Ann, the tragic maid
of local story, parted from her love,
who, forced to marry, broke her heart and died.

We used to walk for miles, in woods and glades,
picking wild flowers on the mountain sides,
climbing the ancient, sturdy, twisted trees
and dabbling hands and feet in burbling streams.

Years later, my mother-in-law confessed
she felt sorry for me. "Why?" I asked, intrigued.
"Being brought up in a coal-mining valley
with all that industry and ugliness."

*Residents of Maesteg, past and present, will recognise
the place names in this poem and will be familiar with
the story of 'The Maid of Cefn Ydfa'.*

On the Morning of your Funeral

It's raining when I leave the B and B,
to walk again beside the angry sea.
The sand, forsaken by the ebbing tide,
lies grey and desolate, a jilted bride.
Bedraggled rooks sit hunched up on the railings
in deepest black - and gulls keep up their wailings,
like women at a wake in bygone years,
while, down the rocks, the waves weep salty tears.
Where the horizon's just a misty blur,
I fancy that your spirit lingers there.
This morning's ramble has been bittersweet.
I'll make my way to church, where friends will meet.
Together we will say our last goodbyes
beneath these woebegone, dejected skies.

*In memory of Jan Reid-Jones, of Llanbadarn Road,
Aberystwyth, 6th July 1943 to 8th December 2017.*

First published in Aberystwyth EGO, August 2018.

Peak District in Winter

As sunshine vanquishes the morning mist,
bare trees stand forth against the cold, blue sky -
such naked grace can almost paralyse
the senses - then the winding, switchback drive
on narrow roads, beside the frost-capped dry
stone walls, embracing silent fields.
High-steepled churches peep from folded hills
and, in the villages, the gardens of
each stone-built cottage, gleaming berry-bright,
are filled with grateful flocks of hungry birds.
Out on the moors,
the lonely, stunted trees all lean one way.
Here, streams abound, and, on the valley floors,
where sunlight's probing fingers fail to reach,
frost lingers, turning grass and bracken fronds
to silver-white.

*First published in 'Landscapes', an anthology edited
by Margaret Holbrook and published by Empress
Publishing, 2018.*

Prospecting

(Leaf gathering in Autumn)

Today, prospecting on the garden's 'beach',
amidst the shingle's multi-coloured hues,
of copper, bone, and opalescent pearl,
I found some amber, topaz, rubies red,
bright silver pence and sovereigns shining gold.
With aching back I gathered up the hoard
and tenderly transferred it, pail by pail,
into the compost – food for next year's rose.

And, while I worked, I thought of one poor boy,
a distant relative, who, at nineteen,
sailed to Australia, where he hoped to make
a fortune toiling in that country's mines
to help support his mother, back in Wales.
Within a year, he'd died, the victim of
an accident - no health and safety then,
no compensation for a life cut short.

Last year, we went, and followed in his steps,
stood underneath a jacaranda tree,
saw where his boat had docked, walked where he'd walked
and viewed the building where he'd registered,

found his death noted in the local press
identified the gold mines where he'd worked -
a long-anticipated visit made,
a thrill for us – and yet, a homage paid.

In memory of David Lodwick, born Tregaron, 1866, died Queensland, 1887.

In October 2017 we visited Maryborough, where he'd docked.

The Letter

"Dear Devi,
Dad is in Sully Hospital.
They are going to operate on Tuesday
to remove half his lung. He has a 50:50 chance.
Can you get permission to come home?
Love,
Mam."

It was Tuesday.
I told my friends, sped to college,
stood before the imposing door
of the Vice Principal's office
and knocked. He was kind.
"Take as long as you like. I hope
your father will be all right."

Three buses, one from Aberystwyth to Ammanford,
the next to Neath – and, all that time
not knowing if he was dead or alive.
No mobile phones, of course,
no way to find the information,
just that fear, all day long -
I might arrive and find him gone.

I think I got the Cardiff bus from Neath,
then got off and hitch-hiked out to Sully.
Bursting through the doors at last, I said,
"I'm Edgar Williams' daughter, Is he ... is he ...?"
"Come this way, my dear..."
and there he was, sitting up in bed.
Thank God, he wasn't dead - at least, not then.

*'Devi' was my pet name within the family. I was at
university in Aberystwyth. My father never had the
operation. He stopped breathing on the operating table
and the operation was aborted. They treated him
with radiotherapy, which killed the cancer for a while
but he died of a secondary tumour, three years later, in
January 1965, when I was twenty-two and he was
fifty-nine.*

A

Touch

Of

Humour

Accident Prone

I've been 'domestic goddessing'
since back from holiday –
the washing's done, the ironing
is safely put away.

The motorhome was caked with mud,
you'd wonder where it's been
but Hub and I joined forces
so now it's sparkling clean.

I blitzed the house and baked some cakes
and then I started flirtin'
with thoughts that it was time to wash
the grubby shower curtain.

I clambered up into the bath
and, though it was so boring,
began unhooking all the rings…
The pole leapt from its mooring!

I felt it go, the fear kicked in,
my little heart was racin'
but luckily I plummeted
into the bathroom basin.

Some paint's come off, a ring has snapped,
the pole is a disaster -
I thought I was uninjured –
didn't even need a plaster

but this morning I've discovered
a quite impressive bruise
upon my wrist, reposing there
in green and purple hues.

I don't know how it happened
but of one thing I am certain,
who else could make a pig's ear
of a flippin' shower curtain?

Advice to Chumps on Lumps and Bumps

Lumpy gravy, lumpy custard –
neither of them cuts the mustard.
Savoury or sweet and milky,
try to beat your sauces silky.

Sand fly bites can hurt like hell,
feet and ankles swell and swell.
'Ere you paddle, don't be mean,
buy some antihistamine.

Midges and mosquitoes bite –
lumpy spots a dreadful sight.
They love dampness so you oughter
spray yourself when near water.

When on woodland walks, take care,
keep your wits sharp, be aware -
ants in pants bring hideous lumps.
Do not sit to rest on stumps.

If lumps on your anatomy,
are found where lumps should never be,
consult the doc without delay,
for swift response can save the day.

So. If you're down and in the dumps
with lumps and bumps and sundry grumps,
use your noddles, don't be fools,
remember these few simple rules!

Pilates Class

I went to a Pilates class -
'twas in the Village Hall.
I thought that it would help me
to stand up straight and tall.

The others found it easy,
being flexible and sporty,
though most of them, I must admit,
were twixt eighteen and forty.

When you are in your seventies
and haven't exercised
for decades, your agility
is somewhat compromised!

And so I puffed and creaked and groaned
while every muscle ached.
"What *am* I doing here?" I thought –
"This notion was half-baked!"

The movements were a mystery;
I got instructions wrong.
Like a beleaguered boxer, I
was waiting for the gong.

And when the class was over
I just yearned to disappear
and hide my shame… Hang on – I paid
a fortune for the gear!

Because 'Scrooge' is my middle name
and I'm not one to quit,
I'll stay to get my money's worth,
perhaps get lithe and fit!

The Fall

Now, if you're sitting comf'tably,
then listen to my ballad;
it is a Summer evening tale
of pizza and of salad.

"I'll take the plates out, love," I said,
for your hands tend to shake,
but I am steadier and I'd hate
the crockery to break.

The threshold proved my downfall – I'm
not sure what happened there,
but suddenly I found myself
in transit through the air.

A plate went flying from my grasp;
I heard a sickening sound
and turned to see the china spread
in pieces on the ground.

My pizza lay in disarray –
condemn me if you must –
I grieved more for my olives which
were rolling in the dust.

Meanwhile, and somewhat overcome,
I lay there in a huddle.
Was I in need of ambulance
Or just a hubby cuddle?

We checked and found me shaken, more
than usually dazed,
but only with a twisted foot,
a hand and elbow grazed.

We shared the unspoilt pizza and
the salad bowl was fine,
but all clouds have a lining so
we drank our fill of wine!

*Published online by The Society of Classical Poets,
March 2018, and, subsequently, in its printed Journal.*

Why?

Why do the birds chirp so loudly
when I haven't heard them since Spring?
Why is the smartphone so rowdy?
What's become of its gentle ping?

Why do my feet clitter-clatter
when crossing the kitchen floor?
Why does the rain's pitter-patter
hammer so hard on the door?

Why does my clock's mellow chiming
sound strident and harsh to my ears?
Why does the Autumn wind's whining
elicit irrational fears?

Why does the kitchen foil rustle
as if to awaken the dead
and everyday hustle and bustle
cause bedlam inside my poor head?

The likelihood is that you've guessed it,
the source of my sorrow and woe –
my hearing aids, long since neglected,
are back where such gadgets should go.

So now I can hear when you're speaking –
you don't have to tell me three times -
but it's quietude's bliss that I'm seeking
and the old clock's melodious chimes!

Writers' Block

It comes as an unwelcome shock
to be struck down by writers' block,
when words that once were wont to flow
are stuck and brain is on 'go-slow'.

I started a Petrarchan sonnet
but spark-plugs died beneath my bonnet
and so my high-falutin plan
vanished quickly down the pan.

Attempts at forms like villanelle
and rondeau did not turn out well.
Even the three-line Haiku fell
a victim to its noxious spell.

I sat with notebook close at hand
and wished my pen a magic wand
but had to reach the sad conclusion
that magic's just a fool's delusion.

I tossed and turned, had sleepless nights,
for how I yearned to get it right!
When every effort went amiss
I ended up just writing this!

Haiku

What is a Haiku?

The Haiku (plural also 'Haiku') is a Japanese form consisting of only three lines containing 5 – 7 – 5 syllables or fewer. It is known as 'one breath poetry' because its brevity enables it to be read in one breath.

The subjects of Haiku are usually nature or the seasons; Haiku are sometimes philosophical and / or introduce an element of contrast or surprise. This can be represented in English by a full stop, comma, dash etc., usually in the middle of the second line.

Japanese Haiku are written without capital letters because the Japanese language does not have letters as such. Many writers consequently choose to avoid capital letters when writing Haiku in English. Japanese Haiku are also written without titles and some of those writing Haiku in English follow this convention, too. However, both these styles are considered to be a matter of choice and my Haiku are written using both capitalisation and titles.

Many writers of Haiku seem to think it is merely a matter of counting syllables - but *the exact number of syllables is less important than capturing the essence of Haiku.* I think of a Haiku as *an attempt to make the ordinary extraordinary.*

Writing a successful Haiku is a much greater challenge than it seems on the surface. It is important that every word is carefully chosen and my Haiku often undergo more revisions than a full-length poem!

Time

Who's Watching?

Time is the name
of the silent spectator
at every game.

Runaway Train

Time is a runaway train
gathering speed as it approaches
the end of the track.

Down the Plughole

Time's gone in a wink,
like the whirlpool of water
that drains down the sink.

On my Shoulder

Time sits
on my shoulder
like a hooded crow.

Autumn

Bridal Wreath

Haloed in soft mist,
my Bridal Wreath stands radiant,
early-autumn-kissed.

Bridal Wreath is the common name for a variety of the shrub
Spiraea.

Birthing

Ready to drop –
damson's velvet-skinned womb-fruit,
softly they plop.

Autumn

Still warm but soon to bed,
she'll lay her golden tresses
beside a hoary head.

'Bridal Wreath' and 'Birthing' were written for the online
poetry course 'Season of Mists' in October 2018.

Freedom

Skylark

The springtime skylark
soars – and pours melodious notes
in joyous freedom.

The Open Road

Ancient motorhome,
freedom of the open road –
quietudes beckon.

Moorland

Heather-covered moor,
haunt of grouse and pheasant,
pathways to explore.

France, August 2018

River Mayenne

Sand martins' low dash,
skimming the water, like
the insects they catch.

Kingfisher, River Cher

Downstream,
dark shape, you flew – turned, caught the light,
flashed blue.

Savonnieres

Relentless heat,
the weir, like a fan,
preventing sleep.

Le Loir at Lavardin

Willows sweep low,
beneath Gothic arches,
river runs slow.

Nature

Tree Stump Cat

I turned the corner.
The tree stump shaped like a cat
spooked me, staring back.

Blackberrying

Blackberries gleam
where nettles spring – the sweetness
worth the sting.

Jacaranda

Jacaranda tree,
your mauvy-purple magic
mesmerises me.

*(Jacaranda trees were in full bloom in Queensland,
October 2017)*

The Somme in September

Privileged

Privileged to give
time - to visit those who weren't
privileged to live.

Morlancourt No. 1 Cemetery

Remote Morlancourt,
mauve Michaelmas daisies,
bright insects galore.

Welsh Dragon at Mametz

Tearing the wire,
watching, where Welsh sons were slain,
dragon breathes fire.

At the Edge of a Field

Piled stones,
some smooth and bleached,
like bones.

Miscellaneous

Tomorrow

Tomorrow,
who will read the lines I write
today?

Windows

Sometimes I can see,
through the windows of your eyes,
what lies in your heart.

Life

Life's a labyrinth
of winding paths, false starts
and new beginnings.

In the Garden in Winter

In the flowerpot,
two dead brown leaves fluttering
like a pinioned bird.

The Muse

Fickle Muse

Today my thoughts crunch-crackle in my head,
crisp as the fallen leaves they zip and zing.
Ideas form in sizzling infra-red
and, soaring like a falcon, they take wing.

Tonight, like Catherine wheels inside my brain,
cogs whirr - and coloured stars go shooting by.
Surrounded by soft sparks of golden rain,
my ready words will rocket to the sky.

Tomorrow freezing fog with icy hand
will fasten on my heart its choking curse,
coil furtive fingers like a steely band
around my throat and suffocate my verse.

How like November you, my fickle Muse,
do your defenceless devotees abuse!

*This sonnet was written in November 2010, soon after I
started writing poetry.*

Feast or Famine

This writing poetry's a crazy scene –
my brain is numb or else it's all aflame.
It's feast or famine. There's no in-between.

It's sun-parched yellow or it's verdant green.
It's past all reason; no-one is to blame.
This writing poetry's a crazy scene.

One day I feel as fecund as a queen,
the next I hang my head to hide my shame.
It's feast or famine. There's no in-between.

Is poetry imprinted in our genes,
success and failure's highs and lows the same?
This writing poetry's a crazy scene.

Sometimes I think I'm just an old has-been
when words emerge pedestrian and lame.
It's feast or famine. There's no in-between.

I wish I were a masterly machine
and churned out lines with ease to high acclaim.
This writing poetry's a crazy scene;
it's feast or famine – there's no in-between.

*This villanelle was written in July 2018, when poetry
came pouring out after weeks of barrenness.*

Cinquains

What is a Cinquain?

The cinquain was originally a French form, of which there are several variations. I use the type developed by the American poet, Adelaide Crapsey, using a syllable count of 2 – 4 – 6 – 8 – 2.

Great White Egret

He preens
showy white plumes;
stiletto-billed, sharp eyed,
on long black legs he bends his neck
and strikes.

Green Woodpecker

Feathered
in golden-green,
red-capped with probing beak,
flight's rise and fall, loud laughing call,
yaffle.

Jay

Bright crow,
Arrayed in pink,
Screecher, baby-snatcher,
with wing's blue flash and black moustache,
dapper.

Autumn's round the Corner

A chill
lurks in the air,
early and late, before
the trees catch fire and the nights
draw in.

*This was written for Wendy Pratt's online poetry course
'Season of Mists' in October 2018.*

Harry

(At Thiepval Memorial, Sept. 30th 2016)

Harry,
we honour you,
nineteen, you served and fell
a hundred years ago today
in Hell.

This cinquain was written for Pte Henry (Harry) Marshall, of the South Staffordshire Regiment, who was killed on the Somme on September 30th 1916 and whose niece, Barbara Hill, née Marshall, lives in Worcester. We attended a service at Thiepval on the centenary of his death.

First published online in the Worcestershire Poet Laureate's Remembrance Anthology, 2017.

Terrorism

and

Tragedy,

Depression

and

Deprivation

Grenfell Tower

How must it feel to know you're going to die
when rabid flames demolish and devour
and leave a mausoleum in the sky?
How must it feel to know you're going to die
too young, and bid your family goodbye,
when acrid fumes constrict and overpower?
How must it feel to know you're going to die
when rabid flames demolish and devour?

How must it feel to try to carry on
when you escaped the blaze but at what cost,
to suffer nightmares which will run and run?
How must it feel to try to carry on,
when much of what made life worthwhile has gone,
with home and treasures, friends and loved ones lost?
How must it feel to try to carry on
when you escaped the blaze at such a cost?

*'Grenfell Tower' was first published in 'The Lyric',
Summer 2017 and received an honourable mention
in the next issue.*

*On the first anniversary of the tragedy, in 2018, it was
published online by Poetry 24.*

Homeless

I had a wife, a home, life was complete,
a decent job that more than paid the bills.
Now I'm reduced to living on the street.

Abrupt redundancy conspired to cheat
me of the role I'd worked so hard to fill.
I had a wife, a home, life was complete.

I thought that it would be an easy feat
to find another job with all my skills
but I'm reduced to living on the street.

For, in the end, I had to face defeat;
depression swallowed me and sapped my will.
I had a wife, a home, life was complete.

Debts escalated and I failed to meet
the mortgage payments. Life-plans drained downhill.
Now I'm reduced to living on the street.

My home is gone, my marriage obsolete;
There's little help or comfort for my ills.
I *had* a wife, a home, life was complete
Now I'm reduced to living on the street.

Hopelessness

My heart's the warp abandoned on a loom,
a fly in amber long ago ensnared,
a shattered vase that cannot be repaired,
a snuffed-out candle in a loveless room.
My heart's a prisoner deep within a tomb;
no aspect of my being has been spared;
my very senses have become impaired;
no glimmer enters to disperse the gloom.

I yearn once more to hear the blackbird sing,
to smell the indoor hyacinth - and see
Spring flowers rising from their icy grave.
I long to taste, in wind's pernicious sting,
the tingling, tangy saltness of the sea.
To feel, to feel again, is all I crave.

*This is a description of how I felt during a period of
depression.*

Manchester, May 22nd 2017

So many lives cut short, so many altered,
the music overcome by screams and groans,
when evil walked unchecked into the foyer
as concert-goers left to journey home.

Some call it cowardice – there lies confusion;
he blew himself up too – that takes some nerve;
the tragedy is in the sick delusion
that Paradise is what he now deserves.

What God with any sense demands the slaughter
of innocents – and all the grief and pain,
each one somebody's son, somebody's daughter
who'll never walk in through the door again?

So many grieving hearts will never mend;
when will destructive hatred ever end?

Published online by The Society of Classical Poets,
March 2018

Silencer

St Valentine's Day, 2018

Children's shrill voices carry on the wind
from the safe playground of our village school.
In Florida, a teen with troubled mind
and far too easy access to a gun
hushed seventeen voices, thinking it was cool,
a silence that can never be undone.

Published online in Poetry24, February 2018

Miscellaneous

Ageing

Thin skin, blue-veined
hands, like last year's leaves,
fragile, dry, skeletal.
Hair, once a chestnut mane,
blanched silver,
like the first hard frost.

Cheeks wrinkle
as apples do.
Bones grow brittle
like twigs that snap
in Autumn gales.
Memory swirls like mist
hither and thither
and cannot be pinned down.

Yet I have lost
nothing - for still
I love, laugh, live,
look forward
to each new season,
each new dawn.

This poem was written for Wendy Pratt's online poetry course 'Season of Mists' in October 2018

Horizons

I saw the far horizon in a dream,
one morning, as the sun began to rise
and fiery pinks and golds suffused the skies
and stained the sea, like pictures on a screen.
I saw the distant line transmute to green
and, as I stared with unbelieving eyes
into the distance where the gannet flies,
mountains and habitations joined the scene.

If, as in dreams, we lose our preconceptions,
converse with those outside our normal sphere,
embrace new challenges and feel no fear,
experience that which now seems strange and new,
open our minds to differing perceptions,
our own horizons may be widened too.

Double Dactyl Poems

'Tales from Shakespeare'

Juliet

Dazedly, crazedly,
Ju-li-et Capulet,
woke up distraught to find
Romeo dead;

picked up his dagger, quite
overemotional,
hoped she would meet him in
Heaven instead.

Othello

Jealously, zealously,
sad Moor of Venice, he
foolishly credited
Iago's vile lies,

strangled his blameless wife
unjustifiably,
guilt and his dagger made
swift his demise.

A double dactyl poem is a poem written in dactylic metre (one stressed followed by two unstressed syllables) following specific rules.

Fading

Memories, that once were clear and bright,
are fading now - a fuzziness
blurs edges. Names and faces
hover just out of sight,
details of places
no longer strong.
Tomorrow
they'll be
gone.

*This poem is a nonet, a nine line poem with nine syllables
in the first line, reducing line by line to one syllable.
The form was chosen to echo the subject matter. It
was written to reflect both my own memory loss and that
of my friend, the late Reg Saville.*

River

I am an individual –
right from my peaty source,
tumbling down the mountainside
I plough my special course.

Alone but never lonely,
I share the bracing air
with moorland birds, the heather,
 the timid mountain hare.

Cascading over boulders
in tiny waterfalls
I hear the new lambs bleating
the buzzard's mewing call

I'm home to paddling children
on days of summer sun,
when dogs delight in splashing
with sticks - and having fun.

Continually changing
on my journey to the sea,
I never lose my selfhood;
quintessentially, I'm me.

Older now and wider
I meander to the coast -
but, when I'm forced to mingle,
my identity is lost.

Rondeau in Pink

In vibrant pink, late Spring display
of cherry trees - the pavements grey
bedecked in petals when they drop.
Hydrangea heads' luxuriant mops
trapped in a vase by Claude Monet.

A candyfloss on holiday,
thrift flower tufts above the bay,
a garish bubble gum that pops
in vibrant pink.

A rosy sky at break of day,
a bleeding heart with arching spray,
a milkshake foaming at the top,
fluorescent socks for jive and bop,
a Summer wine with crisp bouquet,
in vibrant pink.

'Bleeding heart' is Dicentra Spectabilis, a plant with heart-shaped pink flowers and arching spray.

A Rondeau is a poem with only two rhymes and a refrain. The most well-known example is probably 'In Flanders Fields' by John McCrae.

'Rondeau in Pink' was first published in 'The Lyric', Summer 2017

Rondeau in White

In purest white, frail snowdrops bring
the hope that Winter's lost its sting.
The surly blackthorn's starry spray,
the early lambs in prancing play
proclaim the imminence of Spring.

The glimmer of a moonstone ring,
the brilliance of the gannet's wing,
the crests of breakers in the bay,
in purest white.

The barn owl softly quartering
the ground; peace lilies sorrowing;
the hawthorn blossom every May,
cascading like a bride's bouquet
lace-curtained windows revelling
in purest white.

Rondeau: The Mind

The mind can be a flying kite,
embracing freedom, gaining height;
a cauldron bubbling to the brim
with fertile thoughts, a joyous hymn,
a canticle of sheer delight.

A battlefield where armies fight,
a whirlpool on a sleepless night
where jarring notions thrash and swim,
the mind can be.

A soaring larch tree struck by blight,
a glorious pheasant shot in flight
a wasteland, desolate and grim,
a moonless sky, obscure and dim,
a lonely dungeon lacking light
the mind can be.

First published in 'The Lyric', Fall 2017

The Red and the White

Wear the white poppy if you will –
God knows this world is sick of war,
but don't condemn me if I still
wear the red poppy as before.

I wear it not to glorify
the thrall of empire and its might,
nor to perpetuate the lie
that it's a noble thing to fight –

from needless pain on fields of France
to brutal conflicts far and wide,
where minds and limbs stand little chance,
to satisfy imperious pride.

Simply to honour millions killed
I wear the red. I always will.

At the time of the Armistice Centenary on 11th November 2018, many people were advocating the wearing of the white poppy for peace and contending that the wearing of the red poppy glorified war and empire. I wrote this poem to counteract these arguments and to defend my ongoing choice to wear a red poppy.

Voyeur

I snap the self-same view over and over
out of my window, spying on the trees.
I'm privy to their nakedness in winter;
in springtime watch them don their tender leaves.
I see them when respectable in summer
and catch them stripper-dancing in the fall;
I capture changing skies between their branches,
immortalise the warning pink of dawn.
I follow them in every kind of weather;
I know them wrapped in snow and veiled in rain;
I see the sunshine glint on fur and feather –
the self-same view but never twice the same.

*First published in 'The Green Man Alphabet' by
Michael Dante*

Words

"The pen is mightier than the sword,"
someone once said. If it were true,
we poets could, just by our words,
go right back to the drawing board
and re-create this world anew.

The quotation was first used in its current form by Edward Bulwer-Lytton in his 1839 historical play, 'Richelieu; Or the Conspiracy'

Cerddi Dau Dafod

Poems in Two Tongues

I was bilingual until I was five, when we moved to Dagenham and the language of the home changed to English only. Unexpectedly, we were only in England for a few months but it was long enough for me to lose my Welsh. I re-learned it at a later date but English has remained my stronger language and the one in which I normally write my poems. I was, therefore, delighted when three of the poems in this section came into my head in Welsh first and were subsequently translated into English.

I had previously translated a number of poems by well-known Welsh writers into English – one day these may form the basis of another book. Translating verse from Welsh to English was, therefore, almost second nature. I found it more difficult to translate into Welsh those which came to me first in English. I wonder if my bilingual readers will be able to discern the difference!

In all cases I have translated as literally as I could while retaining the same rhyme scheme and metre.

Pa Obaith?

Mae'r eirlys bach fel llusern loyw-wen;
mae'r saffrwn yn goleuo'r gwyll fel gem.
Cyn hir cenhinen Bedr a gwyd ei ben -
ein gobaith wedi gloes aeafol lem.

Â minnau'n gynnes yn fy nghartref clyd -
mae cannoedd yn y trefi a'r dinasoedd,
yn treulio'r nos ar oerni noeth y stryd
o dan gyfundrefn greulon, ddidrugaredd.

Pa obaith sydd i'r rhain, neu i'r trueiniaid
sy'n ffoi am eu bywydau dros y môr?
Ar ôl gweld erchyllterau di-anghenraid,
a erys iddynt ond cloëdig ddôr?

Pa obaith sydd i'r ddynolryw i gyd,
Â ffasgaeth noeth ar garlam trwy ein byd?

Ysgrifennwyd ym Mis Chwefror 2017

Cyhoeddwyd gyntaf yn 'Llais y Derwent'. Haf 2017

What Hope?

Snowdrops, like tiny lamps, are in full bloom;
soon yellow daffodils will light our day;
the jewelled crocus glimmers in the gloom –
our hope that cruel Winter's lost its sway.

Indoors, I'm warm and sheltered but there lie,
out on the streets of many a town and city,
hundreds of homeless, disregarded by
a system that's devoid of any pity.

What hope is there for them, and the defenceless
who've fled, to save their lives, across the sea,
after atrocities no-one should witness
to face rejection and hostility?

What hope is there for all humanity
when fascist thinking once again walks free?

Written in February 2017

Llawenydd yn y Gaeaf

Piano'n seinio'n beraidd ar fin nos,
canhwyllau yn goleuo eglwys hardd,
bedwen yn dangos brigau ceinion, tlos,
robin yn canu gosber yn yr ardd,

ehediad barcud lluniaidd uwch fy mhen,
hen ywen yn cysgodi beddau'r llan,
sidanblu'n disgyn o obennydd nen -
haen eira ansathredig, newydd, wen;

elyrch yn ogoneddus ar y llyn,
perfformiad dawnsio heini a llawn lliw,
aroglau teisen sbeislyd yn y ffwrn,
cerdd sy'n ysgogi emosiynau byw;

cofleidiad, cusan, cwsg bach brynhawn Sul,
y gath yn canu grwndi ar fy nglin.

Winter Joys

Piano music in a twilit room,
Christingle candles lighting up a church,
a robin singing in the winter gloom,
the lacy branches of a leafless birch;

a red kite gliding effortlessly by,
a churchyard guarded by an ancient yew,
white feathers, floating, from a pillow sky,
that first soft coating, still unblemished, new;

mute swans, ice white, majestic on the lake,
lithe dancers, pirouetting on a stage,
the rich aroma of a Christmas cake,
a poem, leaping, lifelike, from the page;

a walk, a hug, a kiss, a Sunday nap,
a purring cat, spread-eagled on a lap.

First published in 'The Lyric', Winter 2018

Y Dderwen

Fi yw'r dderwen.
Fi yw'r brenin.
Rwy'n siarad Cymraeg,
hen iaith yr ynys hon.
Rhoddais fy enw
i Afon Derwent,
i Deri yn Iwerddon
ac i'r Derwyddon
a fuont yn fy addoli.
Fe sathrwyd ein hiaith a'n diwylliant
dan draed y gorchfygwr
ond mae'r ddewiniaeth yn gref
yn fy nghorff, yn fy mreichiau.
Fel nodd yn y Gwanwyn,
byddwn yn codi.
Fi yw'r dderwen.
Fi yw'r brenin.

Cyhoeddwyd gyntaf yn 'Llais y Derwent'
Tachwedd 2018

The Oak

I am the oak.
I am the king.
I speak Welsh,
the old language of this island
I gave my name
to the River Derwent,
to Derry in Ireland
and to the Druids
who worshipped me.
Our language and our culture were trampled
beneath the feet of the conqueror
but the magic is strong
in my body, in my arms.
Like the sap in the springtime
we will rise.
I am the oak.
I am the king.

*Written, first in Welsh and then in English, for
Wendy Pratt's online poetry course 'Season of
Mists', October 2018*

Yr Hen Goleg, Aberystwyth, 2018

Hen Goleg Aberystwyth ger y môr,
fel castell hudol saif ar bwys y lli,
atgofion, ym mhob ffenestr a thwr,
o ddyddiau mebyd – dysgu, hwyl a sbri.

Ar bob ymweliad dros flynyddoedd hir,
rwy'n sefyll uwch y cwod yn edrych lawr
o'r balconi – yn disgwyl gweld, o hyd,
sgarffiau streipïog nas defnyddir 'nawr.

Rwy'n clywed lleisiau drigain mlynedd 'nôl –
ond heddiw mae trawsffurfiad ar y gweill
a bywyd newydd i'r adeilad – rôl
ym musnes, celf, diwylliant a'r lleill.

I'r sawl sydd yn gyfrifol, clywch fy nghri –
peidiwch â sbwylio ein hatgofion ni!

Cyhoeddwyd gyntaf yn Aberystwyth EGO,
Awst 2018

Old College, Aberystwyth, 2018

Old College, Aberystwyth, by the sea,
a fairy castle fast against the swell,
in windows and in turrets, memories
of distant student days I loved so well.

Through the long years, on every visit made,
I've stood above the quad and peered down,
imagining the scarves of green and red
we wore with pride and no-one uses now.

I hear the sounds of sixty years ago –
today a restoration is in store,
new life for the old building – and a role
in business, culture, art and many more.

Whoever is in charge, respect our pleas
and do not desecrate our memories!

First published in Aberystwyth EGO,
August 2018

Dafydd ap Gwilym

'Cerdd Dactyl Dwbl', cerdd ysgafn sy'n cynnwys nifer o draed dactylaidd ac sydd wedi ei hysgrifennu ar ffurf benodol

Llawen ei awen oedd
Dafydd ap Gwilym, a
garodd fyd natur, yr
adar a'r coed;

ffansïodd ferched hardd,
anwrthwynebadwy -
bardd yr Uchelwyr, y
gorau erioed.

anwrthwynebadwy = irresistible

Dafydd ap Gwilym

A Double Dactyl Poem, a light-hearted poem which contains a number of dactylic feet and is written in a specific form

Verily, merrily,
Dafydd ap Gwilym, loved
all nature's world with its
trees and its birds,

fancied the pretty girls,
megadesirable -
bard of the Noblemen,
master of words.

Acknowledgements

Many thanks to the editors of the following publications, where some of these poems first appeared: *The Lyric, Aberystwyth Ego, Poetry24, Llais y Derwent, The Society of Classical Poets, The Dawn Treader.*

Thanks to Wendy Pratt for her inspiring online course 'Season of Mists' in October 2018, for which some of these poems were written. Thanks also to Paper Swans Press and Empress Publishing, each of which included one of my poems in an anthology.

Thanks to my friends in the Aberystwyth Poetry Group 'Diversify'; Friday Poets, West Hallam; 'P M Poets', Derby and those in Isle of Man poetry circles for support and encouragement.

Thanks again to my family and to Barbara Hill, Dafydd Hughes Lewis and Sheila Jacob for believing in me, to Gwynfor Rees for making sure my Welsh was accurate, to Mike for insightful suggestions and to T-Bird for preparing the manuscript for publication. Special thanks to my daughter, Cathy Knight, for the wonderful illustrations.

Printed in Great Britain
by Amazon